NORFOLK'
LIFEBOAT

Picture Postcards

S.B. Publications

Dedicated to all members of the Lifeboat Service who put the safety of others before their own.

First published in 1994 by S.B. Publications
c/o Grove Road, Seaford, East Sussex BN25 1TP.

ISBN 1 85770 054 6

Typeset and printed by Geo. R. Reeve Ltd., Wymondham, Norfolk NR18 0BD.

CONTENTS

Norfolk R.N.L.I. Offshore Lifeboats from 1900.
Norfolk R.N.L.I. Offshore Lifeboat Coxswains from 1900.
Boat Builders.
Acknowledgements.

Front Cover: Cromer lifeboat *Louisa Heartwell* and crew, c.1902.
Title page: Wells lifeboat, *Baltic* and horse team, c.1910.

Royal National Lifeboat Institution

™

25% of all the Royalties from this book will be donated as follows:

15% (10p) to the RNLI
10% (7p) to the Caister Volunteer Rescue Service.

INTRODUCTION

The North Sea has always been a busy seaway with a heavy coastal trade moving up and down the eastern side of England. This trade expanded considerably with the advent of the Industrial Revolution in the mid eighteenth century. Being the age of sail this shipping was particularly at risk to the uncertain moods of the weather and the Norfolk coastline with very few natural harbours on its long length, and with continually shifting sandbanks just off shore, presented a terrible prospect to mariners at times of storm. Bad weather would always mean shipwrecks and loss of life.

To combat this danger the first purpose built lifeboat in Norfolk was placed at Gorleston in 1802, followed by one at Cromer in 1805. These boats were funded by local committees formed of businessmen and gentry appalled by the loss of life that they regularly witnessed. The Norfolk Shipwreck Association was formed in 1823 and took over the few existing Norfolk lifeboat stations, and was then in its own turn taken over by the R.N.L.I. in 1857. These developments helped to organise life saving around the coast into an effective force, and the tradition of the Lifeboat Service as we know it today began.

This collection of pictures is drawn mainly from postcards and concentrates on the offshore lifeboat during the period since 1900 when the postcard became a popular form of communication. The book is intended as a tribute to lifeboatmen everywhere but particularly those who have manned the offshore lifeboats around the Norfolk coast. Men such as Henry Blogg of Cromer, William Fleming of Gorleston and James Haylett of Caister became legends in their own lifetimes. Indeed Henry Blogg, being awarded the R.N.L.I.'s Gold Medal, the lifeboatman's V.C., on three occasions was a world famous figure.

The crews of the lifeboats were and still are highly skilled seamen, and are volunteers. There is no rule that says they have to go when a cry for help is heard, and there is no rule that says they have to come back safely. Traditionally, the crews are members of the local seafaring community. These men know their area of operation better than anyone and are fully aware of its dangers, but they still willingly put to sea to help others, in conditions where every other sailor at sea is racing for port. Thankfully disasters are rare, but the danger is ever present.

There are many faces that appear in this book to which I cannot put a name and I shall be delighted to hear from anyone who has information that adds to the captions to the illustrations or has any postcards or pictures they would like to share regarding Norfolk and Suffolk lifeboats. It is the sharing of information that will ensure that these brave, skilful men and their acts of humanity will be remembered and not forgotten.

Finally, we must not overlook the photographers and publishers who have recorded on film and postcard the events portrayed in this book. Some such as Tansley at Cromer and Sheringham and Burroughes of Gorleston are known, others remain anonymous, but to each and everyone of them special thanks.

Roger Wiltshire

KING'S LYNN
LIFEBOAT PARADE, 1906

Lifeboat Saturday parades were the brainchild of Charles Macara, chairman of the R.N.L.I. branch, St. Annes on Sea, Lancashire; the first such parade being held in Manchester on 17th October, 1891. The Lifeboat Saturday movement quickly spread throughout the country helping to advertise the Lifeboat Institution to inland towns and cities, raising substantial sums for the R.N.L.I., and were held annually until the beginning of the first world war. In 1915, the R.N.L.I. introduced in their place the Lifeboat Flag Day as its main fund raising initiative.

HUNSTANTON
O.N.440 *LICENSED VICTUALLER* (1900-1931)

All three offshore lifeboats to serve at Hunstanton were financed by the Licensed Victuallers. Shown here is the last of the three, a standard self-righting boat being launched on an August Bank Holiday, c.1910. Horses were used to assist the launch at Hunstanton, but this method had problems. On 26th September, 1902, a horse died in the sea whilst assisting to pull the boat on a practice launch. The horse, a six-year-old black gelding, was valued at £70 which the R.N.L.I. paid in compensation to the owner.

HUNSTANTON
LIFEBOAT TRACTOR TRIALS, March 1920

Delays in launching a lifeboat using horses and the success of the caterpillar tractor in the Great War made it inevitable that the R.N.L.I. would experiment with this form of traction. Hunstanton was chosen as the site for the trials because of the variety of terrain provided by its beach. A tractor launch was successfully carried out in seven minutes with only four helpers, instead of the normal ten helpers and eight to ten horses. The tractor used was a 35 h.p. Clayton which could pull the lifeboat and carriage weighing a total of 7 tons 3 cwt at 6 mph over the beach.

returning from a practice launch. J. Bish...
(Jacobs' Series)

BRANCASTER
O.N.332 *ALFRED S. GENTH* (1892-1917)

The R.N.L.I. station at Brancaster was established in 1874, because the 17 miles distance between the stations at Wells and Hunstanton was thought to be too great. The *Alfred S. Genth,* a standard 34-foot self-righting lifeboat, was the second R.N.L.I. lifeboat to serve at the station and during her time at Brancaster she was launched on service 11 times, rescuing 6 lives.

1203 Brancaster Lifeboat

BRANCASTER
O.N.666 *WINLATON* (1917-1935)

The last lifeboat to serve at Brancaster. The *Winlaton,* a standard 35-foot self-righting lifeboat, was purchased using a legacy left to the R.N.L.I. by Mr. Thomas Thompson of Winlaton. She was launched five times on service but did not perform any rescues. Brancaster was a flank station to Hunstanton, where the initial lifeboat tractor trials had been carried out. In 1923 the Brancaster station was also allocated a 35 h.p. Clayton tractor which had been adapted to the R.N.L.I.'s requirements. The cost of the tractor was just under £500.

The Lifeboat. Brancaster.

BRANCASTER
WINLATON SHEETED DOWN

The lifeboat house at Brancaster had been constructed in 1874 at a cost of £270, but in the early years of this century it was found to be unsafe, and abandoned. The lifeboat was left out in the open and the *Winlaton* is seen here neatly sheeted down for protection against the weather. The wheels of the lifeboat carriage are fitted with Tipping wheelplates, named after their inventor T.H. Gartside-Tipping. The plates spread the carriage's weight over a wider area, enabling it to be moved more easily over sand.

WELLS LIFEBOAT.

WELLS NEXT THE SEA
O.N.375 *BALTIC* (1895-1913)

The *Baltic* was one of three North Country 'Cromer' type lifeboats built for the R.N.L.I., all of which served in Norfolk; the *Zaccheus Burroughes* at Blakeney and the *Benjamin Bond Cabbell* at Cromer being the other two. This class of lifeboat had the reputation of being exceptionally safe. The *Baltic* cost £450 and was a gift to the R.N.L.I. from the Baltic Exchange Lifeboat Fund. Horses were regularly used to assist the launch and five shillings (25p) was given to the first man to arrive at the boathouse with his horses after a service call. The horses used at Wells at one time had to be brought from Warham, a distance of two miles.

WELLS NEXT THE SEA
LIFEBOAT CREW, 23rd August, 1905

The lifeboat house and slipway at Wells were constructed at the seaward end of Beach Road in 1895 and cost £550. The crew, who are pictured in front of O.N.375 *Baltic*, are all wearing the cork lifebelts which were general R.N.L.I. issue until 1906 when they were replaced with Kapok belts. At the front of the group, third from the left, is Tom Stacey, coxswain from January 1905 until September 1917. Behind Tom Stacey, and to the right, is his predecessor William Crawford who was coxswain from 1895 until January 1905.

WELLS NEXT THE SEA
UNVEILING THE LIFEBOAT MEMORIAL, 12th September, 1906

The R.N.L.I. established the Wells station in 1869 and the first lifeboat to serve there was the *Eliza Adams,* a 33-foot standard self-righting lifeboat. On 29th October, 1880, whilst on service in a severe north-easterly gale to the *Ocean Queen* of Sunderland, the lifeboat capsized with the loss of eleven of her crew of thirteen. The crew of the *Ocean Queen* were able to walk ashore safely from their beached vessel after the tide ebbed. A monument was erected at the entrance to Beach Road in memory of the lifeboatmen who lost their lives, and this was unveiled on 12th September, 1906.

LIEU.RIADORE.PRESENTING.R.N.R.LONG.SERVICE.MEDALS.C.G.T.WELLS

WELLS NEXT THE SEA
PRESENTATION OF ROYAL NAVAL RESERVE LONG SERVICE MEDALS TO THE COASTGUARD, c.1908

The Coastguard have always worked very closely with the R.N.L.I. to prevent the loss of life at sea. In the early years of the R.N.L.I.'s existence, members of the Coastguard crewed lifeboats. However, instruction was issued to R.N.L.I. stations that the Coastguards' duties ashore were too important to be neglected and that they should not be enrolled as other than reserve crew members. Today the Coastguard co-ordinates the rescue activities at sea and can request the services of a lifeboat. However, the decision whether or not to launch always rests with the honorary secretary of the lifeboat station.

WELLS NEXT THE SEA
O.N.665 *BALTIC* (1916-1936)

Like her predecessors at Wells with the name *Baltic,* the £2233 building costs were met by the Baltic Exchange Lifeboat Fund. The *Baltic* was a 'Liverpool' class pulling and sailing lifeboat, 38 foot long with 14 oars. On 25th February, 1935, she was called out on service to rescue the crew of three of the Wells motor fishing vessel *Tony.* This was the last time that horses were used to assist an R.N.L.I. lifeboat launch on service. For a short time after this date, two horses were left in service at Hastings, Sussex, where they operated the capstan used to haul the lifeboat up the beach.

(Photograph courtesy of the R.N.L.I.)

WELLS NEXT THE SEA
AGROUND ON THE HARBOUR BAR

The motor vessel *Amenity* of London grounded on the harbour bar at Wells on 2nd November, 1933. There was a moderate gale blowing from the north west making the sea rough. The Wells lifeboat *Baltic* was launched and the crew were on duty from 9.45am to 4.00pm when the vessel refloated. The lifeboat's assistance was not required and this incident was recorded as a 'No Service' in the R.N.L.I. records.

WELLS MOTOR LIFE-BOAT
"Royal Silver Jubilee 1910-1935" with Roadless Tractor

Friths

WLS 2

WELLS NEXT THE SEA
O.N.780 *ROYAL SILVER JUBILEE 1910-1935* (1936-1945)

The *Royal Silver Jubilee 1910-1935* was a 32-foot 'Surf' class motor lifeboat designed to operate in very shallow waters and had a draught of less than 2 feet. To achieve this she was the first R.N.L.I. boat to be propelled by Hotchkiss Cone engines, a form of water-jet propulsion. The fitments of the boat were very basic, having no shelter and being steered by tiller. She is seen at the water's edge on her carriage being towed by Case L-type tractor, T32. The crew in the boat are: (left to right) Bowman, 'Roley' Grimes; Assistant Mechanic, Charles 'Loady' Cox; 2nd Coxswain, William Cox; Mechanic, James Cox; Coxswain, Theodor Neilsen.

WELLS NEXT THE SEA
O.N.850 *CECIL PAINE* (1945-1965)

The *Cecil Paine* was the first twin engined 'Liverpool' class lifeboat built for the R.N.L.I. On some occasions the Wells lifeboat had to be taken to Holkham, a distance of two miles to be launched. This resulted in the station being allocated a tractor T59 in 1954, manufactured by Fowlers of Leeds, which could produce 95 brake horsepower. The tractor, which is seen here, was so powerful that the lifeboat carriage had to be replaced in February 1958 because it was literally being pulled to pieces.

WELLS NEXT THE SEA
STATION ON PARADE

This superb postcard of the *Ernest Tom Neathercoat* stationed at Wells from 1965 to 1990, graphically illustrates the number of people who are directly involved at any station with the rescue of life at sea. The photograph was taken in 1979, the same year that Coxswain David Cox, seen centre of the crew group, was awarded the R.N.L.I.'s Silver Medal for the service on 15th February to the Romanian freighter *Savinesti*. The *Ernest Tom Neathercoat* was at sea for 11 hours in a violent north-easterly gale with blizzards and huge seas washing right over the lifeboat. On return to shore the crew were so cold they were unable to walk, and two of them took two weeks to recover all feeling in their fingers.

(Photograph copyright Campbell MacCallum)

WELLS NEXT THE SEA
O.N.1161 *DORIS M MANN OF AMPTHILL* (1990-)

The *Doris M Mann* is a 12-metre 'Mersey' class lifeboat, a fast all-weather type designed specifically to be launched from a carriage. Built by FBM at Cowes, this boat was displayed at the 1990 London Boat Show at Earls Court. Plans to exhibit her on the latest launching carriage had to be abandoned because the floor was too weak to take the combined weight. The *Doris M Mann* was named at Wells on 17th July, 1990 by the Duchess of Kent.

(Photograph courtesy of Eastern Counties Newspapers)

BLAKENEY
O.N.586 *CAROLINE* (1908-1935)

The *Caroline* was the last R.N.L.I. lifeboat to serve at Blakeney. She was a 'Liverpool' class boat and performed a notable double service on 7th and 8th January, 1918 when in a north-west gale and blizzards, having rescued the crew of 16 from the *S.S. General Havelock,* the lifeboat then proceeded to sea again to rescue the crew of 14 from *H.M. Tug Joffre*. She returned from the second service coated with ice, and ice had to be broken in the sea water channel in the harbour before the survivors could be landed at Blakeney Quay. As the younger men of the village were away fighting in the first world war, the average age of the lifeboats' 17 crew was 55 years, including 7 members over 60 years old.

HAULING UP THE LIFEBOAT

BLAKENEY
BLAKENEY POINT

The *Caroline,* shortly after her arrival on station, being pulled up to the lifeboat house which was situated on Blakeney Point some 4 miles from the village. Once the alarm had been raised and depending on the force and direction of the wind and state of the tide, the average time to launch the lifeboat would be about 45 minutes. On 22nd February, 1932, and again on 13th December, 1933, the lifeboat was launched on service but was unable to proceed because insufficient water on the bar prevented her leaving harbour. These incidents, and also because there were plans to place motor lifeboats at the flank stations of Wells and Sheringham, led to the R.N.L.I. deciding on 14th March, 1935 to close the Blakeney station.

SHERINGHAM
HENRY RAMEY UPCHER (1894-1935)

The *Henry Ramey Upcher* was the second of the two lifeboats provided for the use of the fishermen of Sheringham by the Upcher family who lived at Sheringham Hall. The *Henry Ramey Upcher* was built by local boatbuilder Lewis Emery and completed in 1894. The timber for the keel was specially chosen in Yarmouth by the builder and it was said to be "an exceptionally perfect beam of American Oak, without chick, knot or worm throughout its entire length". The *Henry Ramey Upcher* remained in service as a private lifeboat until 1935, and can be seen today at Sheringham preserved in her shed at the head of the fishermen's slipway.

SHERINGHAM
AFTER THE SERVICE

The *Henry Ramey Upcher* was given to the fishermen for their own protection, and she was regularly launched to escort local fishing vessels. A fishing boat is seen here being pulled up the beach following such a service. On 17th February, 1931, the lifeboat was launched to assist the Sheringham fishing boats *White Heather* and *Welcome Home* through heavy inshore seas. The Cromer motor lifeboat also attended this incident. The crew of the *White Heather* were taken aboard the *Henry Ramey Upcher* and landed safely. The *Welcome Home* tragically capsized in the breakers and one of her crew, Jack Craske, drowned despite Jack Davies, bowman of the Cromer lifeboat diving into the sea to support him. Jack Davies was awarded the R.N.L.I.'s bronze medal for his bravery.

SHERINGHAM
O.N.11 *WILLIAM BENNETT* (1886-1904)

The second R.N.L.I. lifeboat to serve at Sheringham, the *William Bennett,* a 41-foot standard self-righting boat is seen here preparing to launch into a very angry North Sea. The *William Bennett* weighed 6.5 tons, making her difficult to launch and she was used only very occasionally on service, the fishermen preferring to use the *Henry Ramey Upcher.* The *William Bennett's* most notable service was on 11th September, 1903 to the steam yacht *Asteroid* in weather conditions so violent that the lifeboat launched with two men to an oar carrying a crew of about 30 instead of the normal 17.

(Photograph courtesy of the R.N.L.I.)

SHERINGHAM LIFEBOAT. J.C. MADGE.

SHERINGHAM
O.N.536 *J.C. MADGE* (1904-1936)

The *J.C. Madge* was constructed to the special requirements of the Sheringham crew and at 41-foot long and pulling 16 oars she was the largest of the 'Liverpool' class lifeboats to be built for the R.N.L.I. The crew regarded the boat as unsinkable and would go anywhere in her. She was the first R.N.L.I. boat at Sheringham which the fishermen used in preference to the private boats. On one service in February 1916 in a raging gale she escorted the *S.S. Villa* of Bergen into the Humber. The boat was away for four days and the people of Sheringham had given the crew up as lost, receiving no news prior to the lifeboat's return due to the telephone lines having been brought down by blizzards.

LAUNCHING LIFE BOAT, SHERINGHAM.

SHERINGHAM
LAUNCHING FROM THE OLD HYTHE, c.1914

Launching the lifeboats from the shore in front of the town had always been difficult and sometimes impossible due to the changing state of the beach at Sheringham. A site one mile to the west of the town was chosen in 1902 and a new lifeboat house built there in 1904 ready for the *J.C. Madge*. To reach the 'Old Hythe', the crew had to race over Skelding Hill which rises to a height of about 150 feet, no easy task in a winter blizzard.

SHERINGHAM MOTOR LIFEBOAT
18·7·36

SHERINGHAM
O.N.786 *FORESTERS CENTENARY* (1936-1961)

The *Foresters Centenary* was presented to the R.N.L.I. by the Ancient Order of Foresters to celebrate the Order's centenary in 1934. A single screw 'Liverpool' class motor lifeboat, built by Groves & Guttridge of Cowes at a cost of £3,569. She is seen here outside the Old Hythe lifeboat house at her naming ceremony which was performed by Admiral of the Fleet, Sir Roger Keyes on 18th July, 1936. The *Foresters Centenary* is reputed to have been responsible for the rescue of more airmen than any other lifeboat during World War II.

SHERINGHAM
ON THE TURNTABLE

A new lifeboat house was built for the *Foresters Centenary* at the west end of Sheringham promenade and was completed in 1937. The lifeboat house was built parallel to the sea and a turntable had to be provided to turn the lifeboat. The *Foresters Centenary* is seen here being turned prior to rehousing. The most notable service carried out by the *Foresters Centenary* was on 31st October, 1956 to the *S.S. Wimbledon* which sunk in a north-easterly gale. Eighteen of the crew were saved and Coxswain West was awarded the Institution's Silver Medal and Motor Mechanic Craske was awarded the Bronze Medal.
(Photograph courtesy of A.K. Vicary)

SHERINGHAM
O.N.960 *THE MANCHESTER UNITY OF ODD FELLOWS* (1961-1990)

This lifeboat, a 37-foot 'Oakley' type was built at Littlehampton by the firm W. Osborne at a cost of £28,500, which had been donated by the Manchester Unity Independent Order of Odd Fellows after whom the lifeboat was named. One unusual service which this lifeboat performed was in March 1962 when she was displayed for fund raising purposes on the forecourt of St. Paul's Cathedral in London. *The Manchester Unity of Odd Fellows* left Sheringham for the last time in October 1990 to be replaced by a relief lifeboat whilst the future of the station was decided. After a review, the R.N.L.I. for operational reasons, decided to close the offshore station in 1992. In January 1994, Sheringham received the first 'Atlantic 75' class inshore rescue boat to enter R.N.L.I. service. This boat, also named *The Manchester Unity of Odd Fellows,* has a top speed of 34 knots and is the fastest type of craft in the R.N.L.I. fleet.

(Photograph courtesy of Eastern Counties Newspapers)

CROMER
O.N.12 *BENJAMIN BOND CABBELL* (1884-1902)

In 1805, a local committee had placed a Greathead 'North Country' type boat at Cromer. In 1883, the fishermen thought that the lifeboat they were then using was unsuitable for Cromer. They wanted a boat similar to the 'North Country' type, which was a good broad boat and allowed the crew to get right up into the bows and stern. The result was the *Benjamin Bond Cabbell*, the first of the three R.N.L.I. 'North Country' (Cromer) class lifeboats all of which were built by Beechings of Great Yarmouth.

The *Benjamin Bond Cabbell* served at Cromer until 1902, being launched 13 times on service and rescuing 26 lives.

CROMER
MACKEREL SALE, 1909

The fisherman on the right selling part of a catch of 11,000 mackerel at 1d a time is John James Davies, Coxswain of the Cromer lifeboat from 1893 to 1902. John James Davies was Henry Blogg's stepfather. The message on the back of this postcard reads: "It is rough here this week, lifeboat went out Tuesday to a wreck on the Haisboro' Sands". The service referred to was to the *Alf* on 23rd November, 1909, the first time that Henry Blogg had been in command following the recommendation from the Cromer fishermen that he be appointed Coxswain. Blogg's appointment was confirmed by the R.N.L.I. Branch Committee on 4th December, 1909.

CROMER
COXSWAIN JAMES 'BUTTONS' HARRISON

Coxswain Harrison retired through ill health in November 1909 after 41 years service in the lifeboat, the last seven as Coxswain. During this period of service he assisted in saving 82 lives.

FOR THOSE IN PERIL ON THE SEA.
COXSWAIN HARRISON.— CROMER LIFEBOAT.

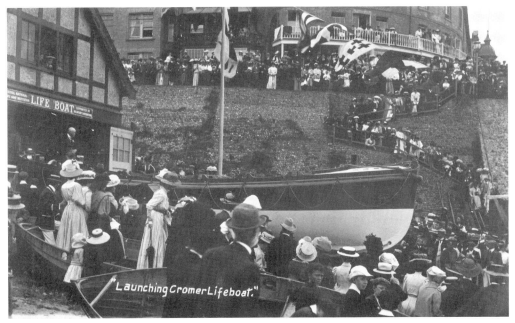

"Launching Cromer Lifeboat."

CROMER
O.N.495 *LOUISA HEARTWELL* (1902-1931)

The *Louisa Heartwell,* a 'Liverpool' class pulling and sailing lifeboat, was built by Thames Ironworks and named on 9th September, 1902 by Lady Suffield, the wife of Lord Suffield, the Cromer R.N.L.I. branch president. The lifeboat house was also built in 1902 at a cost of £652.13.6d, on the site of the earlier house built in 1868 which had been demolished.

CROMER
LAUNCHING THE *LOUISA HEARTWELL*

The *Louisa Heartwell* is hauled down the beach on her carriage by volunteers. There were horses on the beach in the summer to haul the bathing machines, which can be seen at the water's edge. Horses were never used to assist with the launching of the lifeboat at Cromer, there were always sufficient helpers available to effect the fastest possible launch.

CROMER
LIFEBOAT CREW, 1902

The Cromer lifeboat crew photographed in front of the *Louisa Heartwell*. Standing left to right: Walter 'Kite' Rix, Henry Blogg, John 'Pokey' Balls, Tom Blyth, Bob 'Young Dinger' Blogg, George 'Cossey' Nockels, Walter 'Catty' Allen, Bob 'Rumbolt' Balls. Seated left to right: Tom Kirby, George 'Buckram' Balls, Gilbert 'Leather' Rook, Coxswain James 'Buttons' Harrison, John Cox, George 'Old Dinger' Blogg. Seated in front left to right: George 'Bluker' Stimpson, James 'Measles' Harrison, Bob Rix.

CROMER
LIFEBOAT DAY, 1922

The last Lifeboat Day when the *Louisa Heartwell* was the Cromer No.1 Lifeboat. In 1923 Cromer received her first motor lifeboat and the *Louisa Heartwell* became the first lifeboat to serve at the Cromer No.2 station which was then established. The *Louisa Heartwell* remained at Cromer until 15th May, 1931. The crew seen standing are from left to right: Henry Blogg, George Balls, Will Rix, Billy 'Fanny' Harrison, 'Sailor' Allen, Charles Cox, Bob Blogg (in sou'wester), James Davies, Tom Kirby (in chummy hat), Arthur Balls, Walter Rix, Robert Barker, 'Buck' Allen, Billy 'Swank' Davies, Walter Allen, William 'Captain' Davies, Jack Davies.

CROMER
SERVICE TO THE *ST. ANTOINE DE PADOUE*, 29th August, 1912

The fishing vessel *St. Antoine de Padoue* of Nieuport, Belgium, stranded on the Haisborough Sands in the early morning of 29th August, 1912. The crew of 21 took to their own ship's boat and sought refuge on the Haisborough Light Vessel from where they were brought back to Cromer by the *Louisa Heartwell*. This picture was taken in the Red Lion Yard at Cromer. The Belgian crew appear to look very unhappy, but they had lost their boat, they were in a foreign country speaking a different language and they did not know when they would see their home again.

CROMER
SERVICE TO THE *ANN* OF GOOLE, 24th March, 1916

The schooner *Ann* was seen approaching Cromer flying distress signals. Her sails had blown away and she was unmanageable. The *Louisa Heartwell* was launched and on reaching the *Ann* the decision was made to take off the schooner's five crew members having first lashed the helm so that she drove ashore. Shortly after this rescue, the weather deteriorated into a hurricane with a blizzard, conditions in which it would not have been possible to launch the lifeboat.

CROMER
SERVICE TO THE *S.S. PYRIN,* 9th January, 1917

The small Greek steamer *Pyrin* of Pyraeus requested assistance shortly after 11.00 a.m. on 9th January, 1917. There was a strong north-easterly gale blowing and the sea was so exceptionally rough that it was thought to be very doubtful that the *Louisa Heartwell* could be launched. The lifeboat, however, was afloat at 11.40 a.m. but although the *Pyrin* was only two miles out to sea, such was the force of the gale that she was not reached until 2.00 p.m. and her crew of 16 rescued. The *Pyrin* later drifted ashore one mile east of Cromer.

CROMER
WRECK OF THE *FERNEBO*, 9th January, 1917

The rescue of eleven crew from the stern of the *Fernebo* was the first of the epic rescues that made Henry Blogg world famous. The prolonged service to the *Fernebo* followed immediately on from that to the *Pyrin*. Henry Blogg was awarded the Institution's Gold Medal, Acting 2nd Coxswain William Davies the Silver Medal and 12 of the Cromer crew were amongst the very first recipients of the Bronze Medal which had been introduced by the R.N.L.I. in 1916. The average age of the Cromer crew was over fifty. The two halves of the *Fernebo* are seen here from Cromer pier with the beached *Pyrin* on the extreme right.

CROMER
O.N.670 *H.F. BAILEY* (1923-1924)

The *H.F. Bailey* was the first motor lifeboat to serve at Cromer. A 'Norfolk and Suffolk' class boat, she is seen here launching on 26th July, 1923 after being named by Lady Suffield, daughter-in-law of the Lady Suffield who had named the *Louisa Heartwell* twenty-one years earlier. The *H.F. Bailey* was the first lifeboat to be housed at the end of Cromer pier, the boathouse being especially constructed for her at a cost of £30,000. The slipway meant that the *H.F. Bailey* could be launched into sea conditions which would normally prevent lifeboats being launched from the shore.

CROMER
O.N.670 *H.F. BAILEY* UNDER SAIL

Although she was a motor lifeboat, the *H.F. Bailey* carried a full set of sails and oars. The boat was disliked at Cromer and considered to be unsuitable for the station. There were difficulties in launching and rehousing her which were thought to have been caused by the steel on the boat's keel and the steel in the keelway of the slipway biting into one another and causing friction. The boat also suffered from engine trouble whilst at Cromer and on her third service was damaged. She was taken for repair to Gorleston, where she then stayed permanently on service until 1939 after being renamed the *John and Mary Meiklam of Gladswood.*
(Photograph courtesy of R.N.L.I.)

CROMER
O.N.694 *H.F. BAILEY* (1924-1928) and (1929-1935)

The second boat with the name *H.F. Bailey* to serve at Cromer was a 45-foot 'Watson' motor lifeboat. In this boat many of Blogg's epic rescues were carried out including the Gold Medal service to the *S.S. Georgia*. The picture on this postcard could have been taken on 23rd November, 1927 when the lifeboat arrived back at Cromer following the *Georgia* service.

CROMER
SERVICE TO THE S.S. *GEORGIA*, 20th-22nd November, 1927

The *S.S. Georgia* ran aground on the Haisborough Sands in a terrific gale during the night of 20th November, 1927 and broke in two. An epic rescue operation lasting 40 hours then began involving the Southwold, Gorleston and Cromer lifeboats, before the 15 crew on the bow portion were rescued by the Cromer lifeboat at about 4.00 p.m. on 22nd November. Twelve members of the Cromer crew are seen here on Cromer pier following their homecoming: (left to right) George Cox, Jack Davies (Bowman), Sid Harrison, George Balls (2nd Cox), Richard Barker, Jimmy Davies, Jack Davies (Junior), Leslie Harrison, H.W. 'Swank' Davies, Henry Blogg (Cox), Bob Davies (Mechanic), Walter Allen. Not in the photograph is William Davies.

CROMER
HENRY BLOGG PRESENTED WITH 2ND SERVICE CLASP TO GOLD MEDAL

The wholly exceptional nature of the service to the *S.S. Georgia* was recognised by Coxswain Henry Blogg, being awarded the second service clasp to his Gold Medal and the remainder of the Cromer crew being awarded Bronze medals. Coxswain Fleming of Gorleston was awarded the Institution's Silver Medal and Coxswain Upcraft of Southwold the Bronze Medal. Henry Blogg is seen here receiving his award from H.R.H. The Prince of Wales at the R.N.L.I.'s annual meeting held at Central Hall, Westminster on 28th March, 1928.

Coxswain Blogg has now twice won the institution's silver medal, and twice won its gold medal, the V.C. of the lifeboat service. By doing this he has equalled a record which has stood in the history of the lifeboat service for eighty-five years. Only two other men in the 110 years since the institution was founded have equalled his achievement. No one has beaten it.

Jan 1940.

CROMER
HENRY GEORGE BLOGG G.C. (1876-1954)

Henry Blogg was a legend in his own lifetime. He served in the Cromer lifeboats for 53 years, the last 38 as Coxswain and assisted in the saving of 873 lives. This postcard was published in 1934. By the time he retired in 1947, Henry Blogg had been uniquely awarded the Gold Medal of the R.N.L.I. three times and the Silver Medal four times. The dog, Monte, was rescued by Blogg from the *Monte Nevoso* in 1932. Jack Davies, Bowman and then 2nd Coxswain, who took part in all the great services performed by the Cromer lifeboat under Blogg, with the exception of the *Fernebo,* thought that Henry Blogg's supreme seamanship was seen to the greatest effect on the service to the *Mount Ida* in 1939, for which the third service clasp to his Silver Medal was awarded.

CROMER
O.N.714 *H.F. BAILEY II* (1928-1929)

The *H.F. Bailey II*, one of the first twin-engined 45 foot 6 inch 'Watson' lifeboats, permanently replaced the *H.F. Bailey* (O.N.694) at Cromer when the latter was sent for repair to the damage incurred on the service to the *S.S. Georgia*. The *H.F. Bailey II* was not liked by either Henry Blogg or his crew, one criticism being that she rolled badly because "her bow did not make a sufficiently large hole in the water for her stern to follow through". The Cromer crew insisted on the return of their old boat once she had been repaired. *H.F. Bailey II* was renamed *Canadian Pacific* and transferred to Selsey where she did excellent service until destroyed in a Cowes boatyard fire in 1937 whilst undergoing a refit.

(Photograph copyright Beken of Cowes)

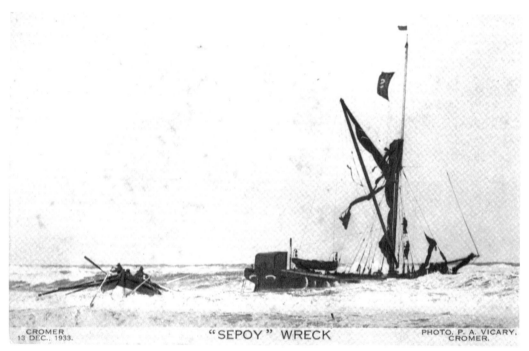

"SEPOY" WRECK

CROMER
WRECK OF THE *SEPOY*, 13th December, 1933

The *H.F. Bailey* was called on service to the Haisborough Sands at 4.30 a.m. on 13th December, 1933. On the same day, another vessel, the *Sepoy* was driven inshore off Cromer by the gale at around 8.00 a.m. The initial rescue attempts were made by the Rocket Brigade, who fired a line to the barge, and the Cromer No.2 lifeboat *Alexandra*. After a great struggle the *Alexandra* was launched, and on seeing that the *Sepoy's* crew were too exhausted to haul in the Rocket Brigade's line, the lifeboat crew used it in an attempt to pull the *Alexandra* up to the barge. The stern of the *Sepoy* had nearly been reached when the line broke and the lifeboat was swept back to shore.

"SEPOY" RESCUE

CROMER
RESCUE OF THE *SEPOY'S* CREW

The *H.F. Bailey* heading for Gorleston, was met in the Yarmouth Roads by the Gorleston lifeboat at 11.15 a.m. and informed of the *Sepoy's* situation at Cromer. Blogg turned for Cromer immediately arriving at 3.00 p.m. Wind, tide and wreckage made it impossible to lay alongside the barge. Henry Blogg turned the lifeboat inshore of the barge, and drove the *H.F. Bailey* twice on top of the *Sepoy,* one of her crew being hauled into the lifeboat on each occasion. Coxswain Blogg was awarded the second service clasp to his Silver Medal for this daring and skilful rescue.

CROMER
O.N.694 *H.F. BAILEY* ON THE BEACH, 1933

The sea was far too rough for the *H.F. Bailey* to be rehoused on Cromer Pier, but the *Sepoy's* crew were suffering badly from exposure and the lifeboat crew were also suffering from the cold. Rather than face a further 28 miles through the gale battling back to Great Yarmouth, Coxswain Blogg beached the *H.F. Bailey* at Cromer. She came ashore on the top of the tide and it took 70 hours of hard work to refloat her. Eleven of the lifeboat's crew are seen here in front of the beached *H.F. Bailey* (left to right): Coxswain Blogg, W. Allen, H.W. Davies (Mechanic), J.W. Davies, G. Balls (2nd Cox), W.H. Davies, L. Harrison, J.J. Davies (Bowman), W.T. Davies, R. Cox and C. Cox.
(Postcard courtesy of A.K. Vicary)

CROMER
O.N.514 *ALEXANDRA* (1931-1934)

The *Alexandra,* a 'Liverpool' class pulling and sailing lifeboat replaced the *Louisa Heartwell* when that well loved boat left Cromer in 1931. The *Alexandra* had been presented to the R.N.L.I. by the Freemasons of England and served at Hope Cove, Devon from 1903 until that station closed in 1930. The *Alexandra* is seen here being launched on Cromer Lifeboat Day, 10th August, 1932.

"SAN FRANCISCO" 9·8·36

CROMER
THE STRANDING OF THE *SAN FRANCISCO*

Whilst on passage from Newcastle to Le Havre, the *S.S. San Francisco* stranded on the Haisborough Sands on 7th August, 1936. The *H.F. Bailey* was launched at 11.40 a.m. that day and assisted the salvage operation until 11th August when she returned to Cromer, there being no further assistance she could give. The *San Francisco* was refloated on 12th August. This picture was taken by the Cromer photographer and postcard publisher, H.H. Tansley, who was taken the 15 miles to the incident by fisherman Robert 'Skinback' Cox in his crab boat *John Robert*.

CROMER MOTOR LIFEBOAT "H.F. BAILEY"

CROMER
O.N.777 *H.F. BAILEY* (1935-1945)

The fourth lifeboat to serve at Cromer carrying the name *H.F. Bailey* arrived at Cromer on 15th December, 1935. She is seen here manoeuvring into position to be hauled up the slipway into the boathouse. The lifeboat house is free standing of the pier, so that if either structure were struck, shock waves would not be transmitted to the other possibly causing damage. Cromer is unusual in that the lifeboat launches directly from the slipway into unsheltered open sea. In severe weather the lifeboat cannot be rehoused and has to go to Great Yarmouth until sea conditions moderate sufficiently.

CROMER MOTOR LIFEBOAT "H. F. BAILEY"

PHOTO
H.H.TANSLEY, CROMER.

CROMER
O.N.777 *H.F. BAILEY* AT SEA

The fourth *H.F. Bailey* was built by Groves & Guttridge of Cowes at a cost of £7,308. She was the first 46-foot 'Watson' cabin class lifeboat built for the R.N.L.I. Powered by twin 40 horsepower Weyburn petrol engines she had a cruising speed of 7.5 knots and a top speed of 8.03 knots. This was the boat that served at Cromer throughout World War II and by the time she left the station in 1945 she had been launched on service 154 times saving 448 lives. The *H.F. Bailey* was returned to Cromer in May 1991 and can now be seen in the Cromer Lifeboat Museum.

SURVIVORS OF SHELLED "CANTABRIA" OFF CROMER WITH LIFEBOAT CREW.

CROMER
THE *CANTABRIA* INCIDENT, 2nd November, 1938

The Spanish Civil War came to Norfolk when the Fascist gunboat *Nadir* shelled and sank the *Cantabria,* owned by the Spanish Government, a few miles off Cromer. The *H.F. Bailey* was launched to investigate the gunfire and rescued the *Cantabria's* Captain, his wife and children, and the steward who had chosen to go down with their boat rather than abandon ship and risk capture. During the rescue the *Cantabria* was listing so heavily that five stanchions on the lifeboat's chain guard were broken by the pressure of the ship bearing down on them. Captain Ardulles is seen here, standing beside his wife and daughter, shaking Coxswain Blogg's hand outside the Red Lion at Cromer, watched by members of the lifeboat crew.

CROMER
O.N.770 *HARRIOT DIXON* (1934-1964)

In 1934, the R.N.L.I. placed the 'Liverpool' class motor lifeboat *Harriot Dixon* as the No.2 boat at Cromer. A tractor was not allocated to Cromer until 1938 and until then the *Harriot Dixon* had to be launched by manpower. Traditionally the men hauling at the front end of the carriage who went into the sea up to their necks on occasions, were paid 'wet money' normally twice the 'dry money' paid to those at the rear who only went in up to their chests. The respective amounts would have been about a shilling (5p) and sixpence (2·5p).

CROMER MOTOR LIFEBOAT "HARRIOT DIXON"

CROMER
HARRIOT DIXON ON THE 'SKIDS'

The *Harriot Dixon* is seen here in the late 1930s being hauled up the beach using 'skids' prior to being returned to her carriage. The members of the Cromer lifeboat fraternity are: (left to right) Frank Davies, Leslie 'Yacker' Harrison, Joe Linder (No.2 Mechanic), George Cox, Henry 'Shrimp' Davies, Billy 'Pimpo' Davies, Jimmy Davies, Jack Davies (senior), Leslie Harrison (senior), William 'Captain' Davies, Henry Blogg, Tom 'Bussey' Allen, Robert 'Skinback' Cox, Arthur Balls, Walter Burgess (tractor driver), George Balls, Bob Davies.

CROMER
O.N.840 *MILLIE WALTON* (1945-1948)
O.N.840 *HENRY BLOGG* (1948-1966)

In 1945, the first forward steering 'Watson' class lifeboat *Millie Walton* was sent to Cromer for evaluation prior to going to Douglas, Isle of Man, where she was to be stationed. The Cromer crew liked the boat so much they asked to keep her. Their request was granted and she was renamed the *Henry Blogg* in 1948. She is seen here on Lifeboat Day 1955, rehousing on a flood tide. Veering ropes are attached to the North Buoys and the boat is drifting down on the tide to line up with the keelway in the slipway. The hauling span is being taken aboard. The *Harriot Dixon* is in the background.

(Photograph courtesy of Eastern Counties Newspapers)

CROMER
SERVICE TO THE *FRANCOIS TIXIER,* 8th July, 1948

The Dunkirk motor vessel *Francois Tixier's* cargo of coal shifted in a very rough sea, four miles off Sheringham. The vessel's list made it impossible for the Cromer lifeboat *Henry Blogg* to get alongside and eleven of the crew were taken off by breeches buoy. The *Francois Tixier* sank throwing the remaining five crew members into the sea, but they were able to scramble into a dinghy from where they were rescued by the lifeboat. The *Henry Blogg* could not rehouse at Cromer because of the sea conditions and is pictured here arriving at Great Yarmouth. The lifeboat crew seen here are: (left to right) George Rook, George Cox (hidden), Tom Jonas, Sid Harrison, a survivor, Jack Davies (junior), Coxswain 'Shrimp' Davies, Bob Davies, Lewis 'Tuna' Harrison, Dick Davies, Frank Davies.
(Photograph courtesy of Eastern Counties Newspapers)

CROMER NO.2 LIFEBOAT, "WILLIAM HENRY AND MARY KING" 6

CROMER
O.N.980 *WILLIAM HENRY AND MARY KING* (1964-1967)

Cromer was the last R.N.L.I. station to have two offshore lifeboats and the *William Henry & Mary King* was the last Cromer No.2 lifeboat. All the 37-foot 'Oakley' lifeboats carried the class number either on the side of the wheelhouse or engine casing with the exception of the *William Henry & Mary King*. Her number should have been 13. She was the last of the 134 lifeboats built for the R.N.L.I. by J.S. White & Co. of Cowes between 1898-1964. She is seen here launching after being named by Princess Marina, Duchess of Kent, on 8th July, 1965.

CROMER
O.N.990 *RUBY AND ARTHUR REED* (1967-1985)

The *Ruby and Arthur Reed* was the second 48 foot 6 inch 'Oakley' class lifeboat to be built for the R.N.L.I. and the first of her class to have a forward steering position. She weighed in total, 30 tons 2 cwt and was the heaviest lifeboat to have been slipway launched, at the time she came to Cromer. On arrival at her new station on 14th March, 1967, she was launched on practice and on rehousing was found to have damaged her port propeller and bilge keel. The slipway had to be slightly modified to accommodate her and smaller diameter propellers were fitted. A busy boat, the *Ruby and Arthur Reed* was launched 125 times on service rescuing 58 lives.
(Photograph courtesy of Eastern Counties Newspapers)

CROMER
O.N.1097 *RUBY AND ARTHUR REED II* (1985-)

The first of the fast all-weather classes of lifeboat to serve at Cromer. The *Ruby and Arthur Reed II* is a 47-foot Tyne class lifeboat built by Fairey Allday Marine of Cowes at a cost of £447,560. She is capable of a speed of 18 knots, more than double that of her predecessor. She was named by the Duke of Kent on 20th June, 1986. On 13th October, 1993, in force 10 winds and sea conditions judged to be the worst experienced by the Cromer crew, five people were rescued from the yacht *Happy Bear* off Trimingham. The yacht was towed into Great Yarmouth harbour, and it was not until 18th October that the sea had moderated sufficiently for the lifeboat to return to Cromer for rehousing. For this service Coxswain Richard Davies was awarded the R.N.L.I.'s bronze medal.

(Photograph courtesy of R.N.L.I.)

LIFE BOAT HOUSE, HAPPISBURGH.

HAPPISBURGH
LIFEBOAT HOUSE

The R.N.L.I. established a lifeboat station at Happisburgh in 1866 and the lifeboat house was built the same year at a cost of £189. After the closure of the lifeboat station in 1926 the house was used as the Coastguard lookout until 1935 when a new lookout was built nearby. After this the boathouse fell into disrepair and was demolished in 1955. Beside the lifeboat house is the Happisburgh Beach Company's Headquarters and in the background the Coastguard cottages and the lighthouse.

Happisburgh Lifeboat

HAPPISBURGH
O.N.580 *JACOB AND RACHEL VALLENTINE* (1907-1926)

The *Jacob and Rachel Vallentine* was a 34-foot self-righting lifeboat designed to an especially light construction by Felix Rubie. This boat weighed only 2 tons 5 cwt, a fact which was probably appreciated by the horses who had to haul her up to the cliff top lifeboat house from the beach. She was launched 16 times on service saving 19 lives, 15 of these being on one service to the *S.S. Edenwood* on 17th January, 1917. This type of lifeboat was known as the 'Dungeness' class, because the prototype was sent to the Dungeness station in Kent.

HAPPISBURGH
LIFEBOAT CREW

The 13 men of the Happisburgh lifeboat crew are lined up in front of the *Jacob and Rachel Vallentine*. The two men standing on the extreme right are teamsters with the horses. When the Happisburgh station closed in 1926, the *Jacob and Rachel Vallentine* was transferred to Palling about 4 miles down the coast which resulted in considerable ill-feeling between the two villages.

HAPPISBURGH
THE HORSE TEAM

A 10-horse team hitched up to the lifeboat carriage with the teamsters in attendance on Happisburgh beach. At one time the team was provided by Love's Farm. Under a provision of the 1894 Merchant Shipping Act the Coxswain of a lifeboat could apply to the nearest Receiver of Wrecks, Inland Revenue Officer, Sheriff or Justice of the Peace, or any commissioned Officer of the Army or Navy on full pay for an order demanding the service of horses. The maximum fine for a refusal to supply horses without reasonable excuse was £100.

LIFE BOAT HOUSE & LOOK OUT,
SEA PALLING.

PALLING
LIFEBOAT HOUSE AND LOOKOUT

The Palling lifeboat station was taken over by the R.N.L.I. in 1857, and a No.2 station established in 1870. The station's close proximity to the Haisborough Sands meant that it was extremely busy. However, the placing of motor lifeboats at Cromer in 1923 and Gorleston in 1924 brought about the closure of both Palling stations in 1930 and 1929 respectively. By that time the Palling lifeboats had rescued 782 lives. Seen here is the No.2 lifeboat house completed in 1899 at a cost of £710. On its roof is a lookout from which the beachmen could keep watch over the offshore sands for ships in distress.

PALLING
O.N.351 *HEARTS OF OAK* (1893-1917)

The Hearts of Oak Benefit Society was founded in 1842. To celebrate the first fifty years of the Society, members throughout the country, voluntarily subscribed to a fund to purchase a lifeboat. The boat was a 'Norfolk and Suffolk' type pulling and sailing lifeboat which cost £416 and was stationed at Palling No.2 station. She was launched 179 times on service saving 190 lives. The Palling coastguards are seen here grouped in her stern. Second from the left is Chief Officer Erridge and fourth from the left is Boatman Bate who was later killed in action while serving in the Royal Navy in the Great War.

Palling Lifeboat Launch.
AUGUST BANK HOLIDAY, 1903.

PALLING
O.N.471 *54th WEST NORFOLK REGIMENT* (1901-1926)

The *54th West Norfolk Regiment* was a standard 37-foot self-righting lifeboat pulling twelve oars, built by Thames Ironworks at a cost of £893. She is seen here being launched on August Bank Holiday, 1903. In a northerly gale on 29th March, 1908, the lifeboat was launched to rescue the crew of the schooner *Vixen* of Fowey which was breaking up. Five sailors were rescued, but a sixth frozen by the cold was immobile tied high in the rigging. James Pestle boarded the wreck from the lifeboat, climbed the swaying mast and brought the man down. For his bravery Pestle was awarded the R.N.L.I.'s Silver Medal.

The Beach Sea Palling.   102960.

PALLING
O.N.656 *HEARTS OF OAK* (1918-1929)

The second lifeboat to serve at Palling and to have been funded by voluntary contributions from members of the Hearts of Oak Benefit Society. Like her earlier namesake she was a 'Norfolk and Suffolk' class lifeboat but was carvel built as opposed to the clencher construction of the first boat. O.N.656 was the last boat to serve at Palling No.2 station and was removed in 1929, having been called out 27 times on service rescuing one life.

WINTERTON
O.N.589 *ELEANOR BROWN* (1909-1924)

The *Eleanor Brown,* a 44-foot 'Norfolk and Suffolk' type lifeboat is seen here on Winterton beach shortly after her arrival at the No.2 station. In the stern of the boat are James Moll (Coxswain 1907-1910) and George Beck (Hon. Sec. 1889-1925). Second from the left, in front of the boat, is Samuel Brown (Coxswain 1910-1919). In 1924 the R.N.L.I. replaced both the Winterton boats with a 'Liverpool' type lifeboat O.N.516 *Charles Deere James.* The local lifeboat men thought that this craft was unsuitable for their work and refused to operate her. The R.N.L.I. withdrew the boat in 1925 and closed the station.

WINTERTON
THE LOOKOUT

Winterton was a village that existed for the sea, virtually all the men finding their living from it. Winterton men were regarded as exceptionally skilful seamen, possibly the best on the Norfolk Coast. There were two beach companies based at Winterton, and the lookout for the Old Company is seen here. The Beach Companies, with their fast yawls, saved the lives of many mariners in distress, whilst also looking for salvage at every possible opportunity.

Caister Life-boat disaster Nov. 14th. 1901. The illfated Beauchamp & Crew.

CAISTER
O.N.327 *BEAUCHAMP* (1892-1901)

A non self-righting 'Norfolk and Suffolk' type lifeboat with a length of 36 foot and a weight of 5 tons. She was launched 84 times on service, saving 146 lives. She is seen here at her naming ceremony in 1892. In the early hours of the 14th November, 1901, she capsized whilst on service drowning nine of her crew. She was never launched as a lifeboat again, becoming a Broadland pleasure craft. It was not until 1st June, 1966, that she was finally broken up.

CAISTER
CAISTER LIFEBOAT DISASTER, 14th November, 1901

Late at night on 13th November, 1901, flares were seen on the Barber Sands. A whole gale was blowing and a tremendous sea was running. It took 3 hours of continuous work to launch the *Beauchamp*. An hour later at 3.00 a.m. cries were heard from the water's edge and on investigating, 78-year-old James Haylett and his nephew found the capsized lifeboat and dragged three of the crew out from under the boat. The other nine crew were all drowned, trapped under the boat. This rare photograph shows the scene the following morning as the capsized boat was pulled ashore.

(Photograph courtesy of Norwich Central Library)

CAISTER
THE *BEAUCHAMP* RIGHTED

The *Beauchamp* had missed stays whilst tacking. She had come ashore and been hit immediately by a tremendous sea on the starboard quarter which capsized the boat, breaking off her masts. The drowned men left six widows and 33 dependent children in Caister. A relief fund was set up which raised £12,000. The boat to which the *Beauchamp* had been launched, bumped over the Barber Sands into deeper water, dropped anchor, rode out the gale safely and proceeded the next morning, unaware of the tragedy in which she had played a part.

(Photograph courtesy of Norwich Central Library)

CAISTER
JAMES HAYLETT

At the age of 78, James Haylett had struggled for over three hours, assisting in the launching of the *Beauchamp*. Although soaked through, he had stayed on the beach, discovered the capsized boat and had then plunged into the tremendous seas on two occasions to rescue survivors. For his gallantry he was awarded the R.N.L.I.'s Gold Medal and this was presented to him by King Edward VII at Sandringham on 6th January, 1902. At the inquest, the Coroner asked James Haylett if there was any possibility that the crew could have given up the rescue attempt. His reply is famously but incorrectly quoted as having been "Caister men never turn back". Haylett actually replied, "No, they never give up. They would have been there until this time if they could have held on. Coming back is against the rules when we see signals like that".

THE OLD CAISTER VETERAN' JAMES HAYLETT

Launch of the Lifeboat at Caister on Sea. Papworth Series.

CAISTER
O.N.431 *COVENT GARDEN* (1899-1919)

This vessel was the second 'Norfolk and Suffolk' class pulling and sailing lifeboat to serve at Caister having been funded by the Covent Garden Lifeboat Fund. The boat is seen here launching from the beach using a haul off warp, which is a rope anchored out to sea which the lifeboat crew can use to pull the boat out through the line of breakers and clear of the shore. After the lifeboat disaster, a new crew was definitely formed at Caister by 21st December, 1901, because at midnight on that date the *Covent Garden* was launched on service for the first time since the tragedy. The *Covent Garden* was launched 153 times on service, saving 166 lives.

Caister Lifeboat, "Nancy Lucy"

CAISTER
O.N.506 *NANCY LUCY* (1903-1929)

The *Nancy Lucy* was the boat that replaced the *Beauchamp*. She was a 35-foot 'Surf' class lifeboat, a small version of the 'Norfolk and Suffolk' pulling and sailing craft. She was presented to the R.N.L.I. by Mr. H.W. Lucy MP, a well-known journalist who wrote for the magazine *Punch*. Built by Thames Ironworks, the *Nancy Lucy* was named on 23rd July, 1903, by Lady Selborne who took two attempts to break the bottle of champagne christening the boat. The *Nancy Lucy* was launched 42 times on service, saving 144 lives.

The Life-Boats, Caister-on-Sea No. 261

CAISTER
O.N.506 *NANCY LUCY* (1903-1929)
O.N.607 *JAMES LEATH* (1919-1929)

The *James Leath*, a 42-foot 'Norfolk and Suffolk' type lifeboat, was originally stationed at Pakefield in Suffolk and transferred to Caister in 1919. At Caister she was launched 23 times on service, saving 18 lives. The *James Leath* was purchased in 1982 by the National Lifeboat Museum in Bristol. She is seen here on Caister beach. On her left is the smaller 35-foot 'Surf' lifeboat the *Nancy Lucy*.

CAISTER
O.N.526 *CHARLES BURTON* (1929-1941)

The *Charles Burton*, a 'Liverpool' class boat was the last pulling and sailing lifeboat in service on the East Anglian coast and her replacement by the motor lifeboat *Jose Neville* at Caister in 1941 signalled the end of an era. Built by Thames Ironworks in 1904 at a cost of £1044, the *Charles Burton* served at Grimsby from 1904 until 1927 and then spent two years as a reserve lifeboat before moving to Caister where she launched 31 times on service, rescuing 15 lives. She is seen here at Caister, ready to be hauled up after a practice launch in 1938.

CAISTER
O.N.834 *JOSE NEVILLE* (1941-1964)

The *Jose Neville* was the first motor lifeboat to serve at Caister. She was the last 35 foot 6 inch 'Liverpool' class lifeboat to be built for the R.N.L.I. with a single engine. The *Jose Neville* was launched 107 times on service, saving 75 lives. She is seen here being launched to lay a new haul off warp. The tractor is T48, a Case LA model which was assigned to the Caister station from 1949-1959.

CAISTER
O.N.978 *THE ROYAL THAMES* (1964-1969)

The Royal Thames was a 37-foot 'Oakley' class lifeboat, and the first lifeboat to be actually named at Caister since the *Nancy Lucy* in 1903. The money for her building was left to the R.N.L.I. by Mr. G.J.F. Jackson who was for 40 years a member of the Royal Thames Yacht Club. *The Royal Thames* was the last R.N.L.I. lifeboat to serve at Caister. To the dismay of the village the R.N.L.I. closed the station on 17th October, 1969. In 112 years of service R.N.L.I. lifeboats at Caister saved 1814 lives, a total unequalled by any other station.

"Shirley Jean Adye" Lifeboat, Caister-on-Sea. Photo: D. Gladwell, Norwich.

CAISTER
SHIRLEY JEAN ADYE (1973-1991)

The people of Caister were convinced of the need for an offshore lifeboat to be stationed at the village and they set to work immediately to provide one after the closure of the R.N.L.I. station. In April 1973, an ex-R.N.L.I. 'Liverpool' type motor lifeboat, then in private ownership and used for fishing at Wells, was purchased by the Caister Volunteer Rescue Service, and brought up to operational lifeboat standards. She was renamed the *Shirley Jean Adye* and ceremonially launched from Caister beach on 5th August, 1973. In her eighteen years of service at Caister the *Shirley Jean Adye* was credited with saving 57 lives.

(Postcard courtesy Don's Supplies, Norwich)

CAISTER
BERNARD MATTHEWS (1991-)

By 1987 the *Shirley Jean Adye* was 34 years old, and an appeal was launched to raise £400,000 to purchase her replacement. Help and assistance were readily given by many people including show business personalities appearing for the summer season at nearby Great Yarmouth. By 1989 the hull of an extended 'Brede' class lifeboat had been purchased and was being fitted out. The great day came on 18th June, 1991, when H.R.H. Princess Alexandra named the new lifeboat *Bernard Matthews,* after the Norfolk turkey 'King' whose donation was the largest single contribution to the appeal fund. The Caister Volunteer Rescue Service has enabled the village's unsurpassed tradition of life saving to continue at one of this country's most famous lifeboat stations.

(Postcard courtesy Don's Supplies, Norwich)

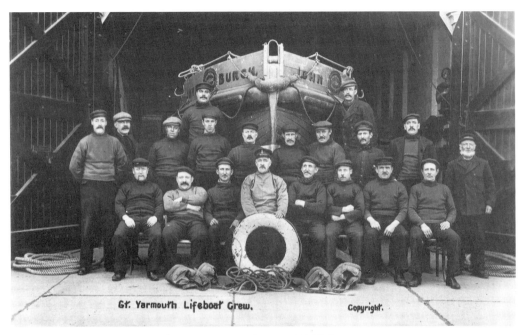

Gt. Yarmouth Lifeboat Crew.   Copyright.

GREAT YARMOUTH
O.N.329 *JOHN BURCH* (1892-1912)

With a length of 32 feet, the *John Burch* was one of the smaller 'Norfolk and Suffolk' type lifeboats known as 'Surf Boats'. She was built by Beechings of Great Yarmouth at a cost of £227. The crew member holding the lifebelt could be W. Brundish, Coxswain from 1902 to 1908, and on his right R. Green, the last Great Yarmouth Coxswain from 1908-1919.

YARMOUTH LIFEBOAT.   Copyright.

GREAT YARMOUTH
ACROSS THE MARINE PARADE

The *John Burch* is being hauled out of the Great Yarmouth lifeboat house which was built in 1859 at a cost of £375. The boathouse stands on the corner of Marine Parade and Standard Road opposite the Yarmouth Marina Centre. After the Great Yarmouth lifeboat station was closed in 1919 the boathouse was used for R.N.L.I. fund raising purposes and housed a reserve lifeboat O.N.541 *James Finlayson*. The lifeboat house was sold by the R.N.L.I. in September 1932 and is today used to house adventure rides for the entertainment of holiday-makers.

LAUNCHING GT. YARMOUTH LIFEBOAT.

GREAT YARMOUTH
LAUNCHING THE *JOHN BURCH*

The *John Burch* preparing to launch into a mill pond calm North Sea. In rough conditions the successful launching of a lifeboat relied on the judgement of the Coxswain. Ropes, known as 'launching falls', were attached to the stern of the boat, and run up to the front of the carriage and then back to the shore. The Coxswain had to watch the waves closely to spot the right moment to launch. On his signal the shore helpers pulled on the 'falls' launching the lifeboat off its carriage. Simultaneously the lifeboat's crew would pull hard on their oars needing to get in two strokes before the boat met the next wave, to achieve sufficient momentum to carry the boat through the line of breakers.

GREAT YARMOUTH
WRECK OF THE *ERNA*, 11th November, 1905

The barque *Erna* of Arendal, Norway regularly carried timber between her home country and Great Yarmouth. In a strong south-south-east gale and heavy seas she dragged her anchor and needed the assistance of a tug. The tow rope parted approaching Great Yarmouth harbour mouth and the *Erna* came ashore on the South Beach and started to break up. The crew of eight were quickly rescued by the *John Burch*. As the barque fell apart hundreds of rats plunged into the sea and swam for shore. At one time the beach is reported to have been black with rats as they raced into the town.

Gt YARMOUTH LIFEBOAT "HUGH TAYLOR" AND CREW.

GREAT YARMOUTH
O.N.629 *HUGH TAYLOR* (1912-1919)

The *Hugh Taylor* was the only 'Surf' class pulling and sailing lifeboat to be of carvel construction. She was also the last of her class, being built in 1912, some nine years after the penultimate 'Surf' boat O.N.506 *Nancy Lucy,* which was stationed at nearby Caister. The *Hugh Taylor* was the last Great Yarmouth lifeboat and when the station closed in 1919 she had been launched three times on service, saving six lives. She was not a hard worked boat. After leaving Great Yarmouth she remained with the R.N.L.I. until 1937, but was only launched a further seven times on service and did not assist directly in the rescue of any lives.

GT YARMOUTH LIFEBOAT. HUGH TAYLOR.

GREAT YARMOUTH
BEACHING THE *HUGH TAYLOR*

The *Hugh Taylor* returning to the beach. The man wading into the sea is carrying the 'casting rope', the purpose of which is to stop the lifeboat swinging ashore broadside with the tide and damaging herself. One end of the rope is attached to the stern of the boat, the other end being held ashore to prevent the boat turning with the tidal drift. From the side that the lifeboat has been approached, it is probable that she has come ashore on an ebb tide which would be moving from right to left.

Entrance to Harbour, Gorleston. 23.

GORLESTON
HARBOUR TUGS

The harbour tugs at Great Yarmouth and Gorleston had always assisted the pulling and sailing lifeboats, often giving them a tow both to and from a rescue. On occasions the tugs would carry out the service themselves. The postcard shows the paddle tug *United Service* returning to harbour towing the Danish brigantine *Anna* which had become waterlogged.

GORLESTON
ELIZABETH SIMPSON (1889-1939)

In November 1888, Miss Elizabeth Simpson Stone witnessed the disaster when the private lifeboat *Refuge* capsized in Gorleston harbour mouth, only three of her crew were saved. Miss Stone donated £500 to the Gorleston Volunteer Lifeboat Association for the building of the finest and largest 'Norfolk and Suffolk' type pulling and sailing lifeboat. The *Elizabeth Simpson* was launched on 23rd October, 1889, and remained in service until the outbreak of the Second World War. Being a private lifeboat, records were not so meticulously kept as for R.N.L.I. boats, but it would seem likely that she saved over 500 lives.

GORLESTON
SERVICE TO THE *WALKURE*, December 1911

The *Elizabeth Simpson* was mainly crewed by members of the Gorleston beach company known as the 'Rangers'. The *Elizabeth Simpson* is seen here at Brush Quay, Gorleston in December 1911 having returned from the Haisborough Sands where she had taken off the crew of 24 from the German barque *Walkure*. Charlie Chilvers, a well known figure on the Gorleston waterfront is seen at the front of the lifeboat to the left of the bow.

GORLESTON LIFEBOATS.

GORLESTON
O.N.288 *MARK LANE* (1892-1921)
O.N.371 *LEICESTER* (1894-1923)

The *Mark Lane* (Gorleston No.1 lifeboat) on the left and the *Leicester* (Gorleston No.2 lifeboat) are here being given a tow out to sea by the *George Jewson*, one of the Great Yarmouth harbour steam tugs. The *Mark Lane* was originally named *Stock Exchange*, having been donated by the Stock Exchange Lifeboat Fund, and served from 1890-1892 under that name at Lowestoft. Her name was changed on her transfer to Gorleston at which station she was launched 298 times on service, saving 484 lives. The *Leicester* was financed from money raised by the City of Leicester Lifeboat Fund. At Gorleston she rescued 89 lives from 72 service launches. This superb postcard was published by F.S. Burroughes of Gorleston. A Kirkcaldy 'Fifie' herring boat is seen in the middle ground with its massive lugsail set and a barquentine under full sail is viewed in the distance.

GORLESTON
O.N.420 *JAMES STEVENS No.3* (1903-1908)

The *James Stevens No.3* was the second steam lifeboat to serve at Gorleston. She was built in 1898 by J.S. White & Co. at Cowes, and had a single propeller driven by a compound inverted engine. She had to be ready to steam immediately at all times. Her Coxswain, Sidney 'Sparks' Harris, won the first of his five R.N.L.I. Silver Medals in the *James Stevens No.3* when the crew of six of the Lowestoft brig *Celerity* were rescued on 15th January, 1905. The rapid development of the marine internal combustion engine in the early 1900s meant that only six steam lifeboats were built for the R.N.L.I. The *James Stevens No.3* was, in 1928, the last to be withdrawn from service, being stationed at Holyhead at that time.
(Photograph courtesy of R.N.L.I.)

GORLESTON
O.N.663 *JOHN AND MARY MEIKLAM OF GLADSWOOD* (1921)
AGNES CROSS, LOWESTOFT (1921-1939)

Lifeboat O.N.663 named the *John and Mary Meiklam of Gladswood* was the first internal combustion engined motor lifeboat to be sent to a Norfolk station, arriving at Gorleston in 1921. There was an immediate dispute concerning her at Gorleston, arising from a reluctance by the Coxswain and crew to appoint an assistant mechanic and the station refused to accept the boat. The *John and Mary Meiklam* was sent to Lowestoft initially on a temporary basis, but the transfer was made permanent in May 1922 and she was renamed *Agnes Cross*. It was this boat that completed the epic rescue of the crew of 24 of the *S.S. Hopelyn* aground on Scroby Sands in October 1922, for which both Coxswain Swan of Lowestoft and Coxswain Fleming of Gorleston were awarded the R.N.L.I.'s Gold Medal.

(Photograph courtesy of R.N.L.I.)

LOWESTOFT LIFEBOAT & FISH MARKET.

GORLESTON
O.N.543 *KENTWELL* (1922-1924)

When O.N.663 *John and Mary Meiklam of Gladswood* was temporarily transferred to Lowestoft in 1921, the Gorleston No.1 and No.2 lifeboat stations were closed by the R.N.L.I. In 1922, when the transfer was made permanent, the Gorleston station was then reopened with the Lowestoft pulling and sailing lifeboat *Kentwell* being moved up the coast. William Fleming was appointed as the new Gorleston coxswain at this time. The *Kentwell* is seen here during her time at Lowestoft where she was stationed from 1905-1921. In October 1922, shortly after arriving at Gorleston, this lifeboat with Coxswain Fleming in command, made the initial gallant attempts to rescue the crew of the *S.S. Hopelyn,* paving the way for the ultimate success achieved by the Lowestoft motor lifeboat.

GORLESTON
GORLESTON LIFEBOAT CREW, c.1923

The mystery of this picture is why the lifeboat crew are wearing cork lifejackets which had been superseded by Kapok some 20 years earlier in 1906? Back row (left to right): Jimmy Stubbs, 'Parson' Woods, Tom Morley, Ernie Stubbs, 'Truffy' Leggatt. Centre: Ted Bensley, Best, 'Sooty Dick' Spurgeon, Walter High, 'Tupp' Gooch, 'Coddy' Harris, 'Dollar' Leggatt, 'Looty' Newson, Billy Halfnight. Front row: 'Crimo' Crisp, 'Jumbo' Fleming, Ellery Harris, Charlie Chilvers, William Fleming (Coxswain), Sam Parker (2nd Cox), Charles Johnson, Harris, unknown. When Coxswain William Fleming retired in 1934 he was credited with having helped to save 1188 lives from shipwreck alone, and had been awarded Gold, Silver and Bronze medals by the R.N.L.I.

GORLESTON
O.N.670 *JOHN AND MARY MEIKLAM OF GLADSWOOD* (1924-1939)

The first *H.F. Bailey* thought to be unsuitable at Cromer was transferred in 1924 to Gorleston and renamed the *John and Mary Meiklam of Gladswood.* She served as the No.1 boat at Gorleston until 1939 and then remained in store there as part of the R.N.L.I. reserve fleet until 1946. A well-liked boat at Gorleston, she was launched 155 times on service, saving 211 lives. She is seen here returning from a service prior to 1926 and is tieing up to a drifter alongside Brush Quay, Gorleston. The Bowman is Charlie Chilvers and next to him are Billy Parker and Cyril Bensley.

Gorleston Motor Life Boat

GORLESTON
SERVICE TO *S.S. FOX*, 27th November, 1924

The R.N.L.I. service report for this incident states that Coxswain Fleming, with over forty years experience, said that the sea on the harbour bar this day was the heaviest that he had experienced for years. In the force 9 gale the size of the seas can be judged when it is taken into account that the picture is taken from well inside the harbour mouth and is one hour into the ebb tide. The *John and Mary Meiklam* had escorted the small Hull steamer *S.S. Fox* from a position of some danger to safe anchorage in the roadstead opposite Great Yarmouth, as it was too rough for the ship to enter harbour.

GORLESTON
JOHN AND MARY MEIKLAM ENTERS HARBOUR

This photograph was taken after the *John and Mary Meiklam of Gladswood* had been rebuilt with weather protection in 1934. The boat was built by J.S. White and Co., Cowes, using only the very best wood – Honduras Mahogany for the hull and decks, Canadian Rock Elm for the timber frames, bilge keels and gunwales, Indian Teak for the keel, English Oak for the dowsings, stem and stern posts and Norwegian Pine for the masts and spars. When she was sold out of service in 1952 she was bought by British Rail Ferries at Fishguard for use as a harbour boat. In 1986 she was bought from British Rail for £5 and returned to Gorleston where she is now being lovingly restored.

(Photograph courtesy of R.N.L.I.)

GT. YARMOUTH & GORLESTON LIFEBOAT
R.N.L.B. LOUISE STEPHENS

GORLESTON
O.N.820 *LOUISE STEPHENS* (1939-1967)

It was originally planned that the *John and Mary Meiklam of Gladswood* should have been replaced as No.1 lifeboat at Gorleston in 1938, but, in altering the Gorleston slipway to accommodate the new boat, it was built 6 inches higher than it should have been and had to be taken up and relaid. The *Louise Stephens* arrived in 1939 and all the preparations were put in place to christen her in the September. The outbreak of war intervened and this boat never was christened. The *Louise Stephens* was very similar to the 46-foot 'Watson' lifeboats but formed a sub class known as the 'Gorleston' type and could not be launched from any slipway other than Gorleston.

(Postcard copyright courtesy Ford Jenkins, Lowestoft)

"Khami" Class 44 Lifeboat.

Photo: D. W. Fletcher, Norwich.

GORLESTON
O.N.1002 *KHAMI* (1967-1980)

In 1964, the R.N.L.I. obtained a 44-foot steel lifeboat from the United States Coastguard for evaluation. The trials were successful and the 44-foot 'Waveney' class was developed, the first six of which, including the *Khami,* were built by Brooke Marine at Lowestoft. This class was the first of the new generation of high speed all-weather lifeboats. The *Khami,* built at a cost of £33,361, was named after a place in Zimbabwe for which Mr. and Mrs. T.G. Bedwell, who donated the money for her purchase, had a particular affection. A noteable service carried out by this boat was on 13th December, 1974, when six people were taken off the *M.V. Biscaya* in a force 9 gale. For this rescue Coxswain Jack Bryan was awarded a bar to his Bronze Medal.

(Postcard courtesy of Don's Supplies, Norwich)

GORLESTON
O.N.1065 *BARHAM* (1980-)

The second 44-foot 'Waveney' class lifeboat to serve at Gorleston. She is named after the battleship *H.M.S. Barham*, sunk in November 1941 with the loss of 859 crew, one of whom was the only brother of Mr. Colin Stringer who left a legacy to the R.N.L.I. for the purchase of a lifeboat as a memorial. The *Barham* was built by Fairey Allday Marine, Cowes, at a cost of £260,000 and is seen here in 1983 at the start of the Tall Ships Race.
(Postcard copyright courtesy of Brian Ollington, Gorleston)

SOUTHWOLD
O.N.691 *MARY SCOTT* (1925-1940)

The *Mary Scott* is the only lifeboat in this book not to have served at a Norfolk station, but she did take part in the service to the *S.S. Georgia* in November 1927. The day before the *Georgia* incident, the Lowestoft lifeboat had been damaged on service. The *Mary Scott* was therefore called to support the Gorleston and Cromer boats. Well outside his own area of operation and not knowing that the *Georgia's* crew had been rescued, Coxswain Upcraft took the *Mary Scott* onto the Haisborough Sands at night, right up to the wreck before establishing that no survivors were still on board. One piece of advice that Norfolk coxswains, on retiring, have always impressed on their successors is: "Never go onto the sands in the dark". For his heroic act Coxswain Upcraft was awarded the R.N.L.I.'s Bronze Medal.

NORFOLK R.N.L.I. OFFSHORE LIFEBOATS FROM 1900

R.N.L.I OFFICIAL NUMBER	NAME	DATES AT STATION	TYPE	BUILDER	COST
HUNSTANTON					
O.N.169	Licensed Victualler	1887-1900	Standard 34ft SR, 10 oars	Woolfe	£336
O.N.440	Licensed Victualler	1900-1931	Standard 35ft SR, 10 oars	Thames Ironworks	£784
BRANCASTER					
O.N.332	Alfred S. Genth	1892-1917	Standard 34ft SR, 10 oars	McAlister	£373
O.N.666	Winlaton	1917-1935	Standard 35ft SR, 10 oars	S.E. Saunders	unknown
WELLS					
O.N.375	Baltic	1895-1913	NC (Cromer) 35ft 3ins NSR, 14 oars	Beeching	£450
O.N.425	James Stevens No.8	1913-1916	Liverpool 35ft NSR, 12 oars	Beeching	£544
O.N.665	Baltic	1916-1936	Liverpool 38ft NSR, 14 oars	S.E. Saunders	£2,233
O.N.780	Royal Silver Jubilee 1910-1935	1936-1945	Surf motor 32ft	Groves & Guttridge	£2,919
O.N.850	Cecil Paine	1945-1965	Liverpool motor 35ft 6ins	Groves & Guttridge	£7,462
O.N.982	Ernest Tom Neathercoat	1965-1990	Oakley 37ft	Osborne	£34,000
O.N.1161	Doris M. Mann of Ampthill	1990-	Mersey 12 metres	FBM	£468,200
BLAKENEY					
O.N.318	Zaccheus Burroughes	1891-1908	NC (Cromer) 35ft 3ins NSR, 14 oars	Beeching	£426
O.N.586	Caroline	1908-1935	Liverpool 38ft NSR, 14 oars	Thames Ironworks	£1,202
SHERINGHAM					
O.N.11	William Bennett	1886-1904	Standard 41ft 4ins SR, 14 oars	Forrestt	£501
O.N.536	J.C. Madge	1904-1936	Liverpool 41ft NSR, 16 oars	Thames Ironworks	£1,436
O.N.786	Foresters Centenary	1936-1961	Liverpool motor 35ft 6ins	Groves & Guttridge	£3,569
O.N.960	The Manchester Unity of Oddfellows	1961-1990	Oakley 37ft	Osborne	£28,500
O.N.986	Lloyds II (Relief Station Boat)	1990-1992	Oakley 37ft	Morris & Lorimer	£34,000

CROMER

ORIGINAL STATION AND NO.2 STATION FROM 1923

O.N.12	Benjamin Bond Cabbell	1884-1902	NC (Cromer) 35ft NSR, 14 oars	Beeching	£365
O.N.495	Louisa Heartwell	1902-1931	Liverpool 38ft NSR, 14 oars	Thames Ironworks	£982
O.N.514	Alexandra	1931-1934	Liverpool 35ft NSR, 14 oars	Thames Ironworks	£945
O.N.770	Harriot Dixon	1934-1964	Liverpool motor 35ft 6ins	Groves & Guttridge	£3,317
O.N.980	William Henry & Mary King	1964-1967	Oakley 37ft	J.S. White	£33,000

NO.1 STATION

O.N.670	H.F. Bailey	1923-1924	N&S motor 46ft 6ins	J.S. White	£10,993
O.N.694	H.F. Bailey	1924-1928	Watson motor 45ft	J.S. White	£7,580
		1929-1935			
O.N.714	H.F. Bailey II	1928-1929	Watson motor 45ft 6ins	S.E. Saunders	£8,470
O.N.777	H.F. Bailey	1935-1945	Watson motor 46ft	Groves & Guttridge	£7,308
O.N.840	Henry Blogg	1945-1966	Watson motor 46ft Forward Steering	Sussex Yacht Co.	£15,245
O.N.990	Ruby & Arthur Reed	1967-1985	Oakley 48ft 6ins	W. Osborne	£60,000
O.N.1097	Ruby & Arthur Reed II	1985-	Tyne 47ft	Fairey Allday Marine	£447,560

HAPPISBURGH

O.N.140	Huddersfield	1887-1906	Standard 34ft SR, 10 oars	Forrestt	£406
O.N.455	Forester (Relief Lifeboat)	1906-1907	Rubie 34ft SR, 10 oars	Thames Ironworks	£712
O.N.580	Jacob & Rachel Vallentine	1907-1926	Rubie 34ft SR, 10 oars	Thames Ironworks	£730

PALLING

NO.1 STATION

O.N.13	Good Hope	1884-1900	Standard 37ft SR, 12 oars	Woolfe	£392
O.N.265	Quiver No.1	1900-1901	Standard 37ft SR, 12 oars	Woolfe	£430
O.N.471	54th West Norfolk Regiment	1901-1926	Standard 37ft SR, 12 oars	Thames Ironworks	£893
O.N.580	Jacob & Rachel Vallentine	1926-1930	Rubie 34ft SR, 10 oars	Thames Ironworks	£730

NO.2 STATION

O.N.351	Hearts of Oak	1893-1917	N&S 40ft NSR, 14 oars	Ellis	£416
O.N.270	Reserve No.1	1917-1918	N&S 44ft NSR, 12 oars	Beeching	£368
O.N.656	Hearts of Oak	1918-1929	N&S 40ft NSR, 12 oars	Summers & Payne Completed by S.E. Saunders	unknown

WINTERTON

NO.1 STATION

O.N.397	Edward Birkbeck	1896-1924	N&S Surf 34ft NSR, 12 oars	Beeching	£436
O.N.516	Charles Deere James (Reserve Station Boat)	1924-1925	Liverpool 38ft NSR, 10 oars	Thames Ironworks	£1,054

NO.2 STATION

O.N.233	Margaret	1899-1907	N&S 44ft NSR, 12 oars	Beeching	£315
O.N.270	Reserve No.1	1907-1909	N&S 44ft NSR, 12 oars	Beeching	£368
O.N.589	Eleanor Brown	1909-1924	N&S 44ft 6 ins NSR, 12 oars	Thames Ironworks	£2,023

CAISTER

NO.1 STATION

O.N.431	Covent Garden	1899-1919	N&S 40ft NSR, 12 oars	Thames Ironworks	£1,295
O.N.607	James Leath	1919-1929	N&S 42ft NSR, 12 oars	Thames Ironworks	£1,934

CAISTER

NO.2 STATION

O.N.327	Beauchamp	1892-1901	N&S 36ft NSR, 12 oars	Critten	£266
O.N.506	Nancy Lucy	1903-1929	N&S Surf 35ft NSR, 12 oars	Thames Ironworks	£1,603
O.N.526	Charles Burton	1929-1941	Liverpool 38ft NSR, 14 oars	Thames Ironworks	£1,044
O.N.834	Jose Neville	1941-1964	Liverpool motor 35ft 6ins	Groves & Guttridge	£4,474
O.N.978	The Royal Thames	1964-1969	Oakley 37ft	J.S. White	£31,749

GREAT YARMOUTH

O.N.329	John Burch	1892-1912	N&S Surf 32ft NSR, 12 oars	Beeching	£227
O.N.629	Hugh Taylor	1912-1919	N&S Surf 34ft NSR, 12 oars	Thames Ironworks	£1,250

GORLESTON

NO.1 STATION

O.N.288	Mark Lane	1892-1921	N&S 46ft NSR, 14 oars	Ellis	£373
O.N.663	John & Mary Meiklam of Gladswood (Transferred to Lowestoft & renamed Agnes Cross)	1921	N&S motor 46ft 6ins	S.E. Saunders	£8,620
O.N.543	Kentwell	1922-1924	N&S 46ft NSR, 14 oars	Thames Ironworks	£2,197
O.N.670	John & Mary Meiklam of Gladswood	1924-1939	N&S motor 46ft 9ins	J.S. White	£10.993
O.N.820	Louise Stephens	1939-1967	Watson 46ft motor	J.S. White	£9,351
O.N.1002	Khami	1967-1980	Waveney 44ft 10ins	Brooke Marine	£33,361
O.N.1065	Barham	1980-	Waveney 44ft 10ins	Fairey Allday Marine	£260,000

NO.2 STATION

O.N.371	Leicester	1894-1923	N&S Surf 31ft NSR, 12 oars	Critten	£328
O.N.541	James Finlayson	1923-1924	Watson 35ft NSR, 10 oars	Thames Ironworks	£1,247

GORLESTON

NO.3 STATION

O.N.326	Thora Zelma	1892-1904	N&S Surf 31ft NSR, 12 oars	Beeching	£231

NO.4 STATION

O.N.420	James Stevens No.3	1903-1908	Steam 56ft	J.S. White	£3,298

PRIVATE LIFEBOATS

SHERINGHAM

Henry Ramey Upcher	1894-1935	34ft 9ins 16 oars	L. Emery	£150?

CAISTER VOLUNTEER RESCUE SERVICE

Shirley Jean Adye	1973-1991	Liverpool motor 35ft 6ins	Groves & Guttridge	£14,398
Bernard Matthews	1991-	Lochin 38ft 6ins	Lochin Marine (hull) Goodchild Marine (fitting out)	£400,000

GORLESTON VOLUNTEER LIFEBOAT

Elizabeth Simpson	1889-1939	N&S 48ft	Beeching	£500

Abbreviations:

NSR – Non Self Righting   NC – North Country   N&S – Norfolk and Suffolk
O.N. – R.N.L.I. Official Number   SR – Self Righting.

NORFOLK R.N.L.I. OFFSHORE LIFEBOAT COXSWAINS FROM 1900

HUNSTANTON

William Petherick	1898-1903
John Riches	1903-1931 (Station closed)

BRANCASTER

Robert Loose	1898-1908
William Loose	1908-1935 (Station closed)

WELLS

William Crawford	1895-1905
Thomas Stacey	1905-1917
William Grimes	1917-1933
Theodor Neilsen	1933-1947
William Cox	1947-1959
David Cox	1960-1986
Anthony Jordan	1986-1989
Graham Walker	1989-

BLAKENEY

George Long	1896-1920
Herbert Long	1920-1935 (Station closed)

SHERINGHAM

W. Bishop	1897-1914
Obadiah Cooper	1914-1924
Jimmy Dumble	1924-1947
J. Hardingham	1947-1950
Henry 'Downtide' West	1951-1962
Henry 'Joyful' West	1963-1984
Jack West	1985-1986
Brian Pegg	1986-1989
Clive Rayment	1989-1992 (Station closed)

CROMER
Original Station and No.2 Station from 1923

John James Davies	1893-1902
James Harrison	1902-1909
Henry Blogg	1909-1947
James Davies	1947-1953
Lewis Harrison	1953-1967 (Station closed)

CROMER NO.1 STATION

Henry Blogg	1923-1947
Henry Davies	1947-1976
Richard Davies	1976-

HAPPISBURGH

Harvey Cannon	1898-1921
John Lawson	1922-1926 (Station closed)

PALLING

James Dane	1899-1913
Denis Popay	1913-1930 (Station closed)

WINTERTON

James Waite	1898-1906
James Moll	1907-1910
Samuel Brown	1910-1919
Walter Dyble	1920-1925 (Station closed)

CAISTER

James Haylett	1888-1900
Aaron Haylett	1900-1901
John Brown	1902-1903
John Haylett	1903-1919
Charles Laycock	1919-1935
Joseph Woodhouse	1935-1950
James Brown	1950-1956
John Plummer	1956-1969 (Station closed)

GREAT YARMOUTH

J. Sutton	1892-1902
W. Brundish	1902-1908
R. Green	1908-1919 (Station closed)

GORLESTON NO.1 STATION

E. Woods	1882-1903
S.J. Harris	1903-1921
W.G. Fleming	1922-1934
C.A. Johnson	1934-1946
W.H. Parker	1947-1949
B.H. Beavers	1949-1954
P.O. Williment	1954-1958
G.F. Mobbs	1958-1966
P. Beavers	1966-1967
J. Bryan	1967-1976
R.J. Hawkins	1976-

GORLESTON NO.2 STATION

J. Bensley	1898-1921

GORLESTON NO.3 STATION

S.J. Harris	1892-1903
(Transferred to No. 1 Station)	
C.D. Palmer	1903-1904

BOAT BUILDERS

Beeching	Great Yarmouth	Lochin Marine	Rye
Brooke Marine	Lowestoft	McAlister	Dumbarton
Critten	Great Yarmouth	Morris and Lorimer	Sandbank
Ellis	Lowestoft	W. Osborne	Littlehampton
Emery	Sheringham	S.E. Saunders	Cowes
Fairey Allday Marine	Cowes	Summers and Payne	Southampton
FBM	Cowes	Sussex Yacht Co.	Shoreham
Forrestt	Limehouse	Thames Ironworks	Blackwall
Goodchild Marine	Great Yarmouth	J.S. White	Cowes
Groves & Guttridge	Cowes	Woolfe	Shadwell

ACKNOWLEDGEMENTS

I would like to record my grateful thanks to those who have shared their memories and experiences with me particularly Henry 'Shrimp' Davies of Cromer, Jack and David Woodhouse of Caister, George Mobbs of Gorleston and Graham Walker of Wells. Barry Cox at R.N.L.I. Headquarters has also been a friend to whom nothing has been too much trouble.

I am also grateful to the following for their help and encouragement:

The Cromer Museum
Alan Atherton, Chief Librarian (retired), Eastern Counties Newspapers
The Maritime Museum, Great Yarmouth
The Norwich Central Library Local History Department
Gerald Cubitt
Dennis Cross
Members of the Norfolk Postcard Club
The Lifeboat Enthusiasts Society
Steve Benz for editing and marketing
and many others not mentioned by name.

The following have either lent me photographs or postcards to include or have allowed me to publish pictures for which they have copyright. I am indebted to all of them.

Philip Standley	pages 12, 69	Campbell MacCallum	page 15
A.K. Vicary	pages 25, 47	Peter Allard	page 77
R.N.L.I.	pages 11, 21, 39, 59, 92, 93, 98	Eastern Counties Newspapers	pages 16, 26, 55, 56, 58
Beken of Cowes	page 44	Norwich Central Library	pages 71, 72
Mark Roberts	pages 80, 100, 101	Don's Supplies, Norwich	pages 80, 81, 100
Ford Jenkins, Lowestoft	page 99	Brian Ollington, Gorleston	page 101

Finally I wish to thank my wife Sarah for having typed the text and for all her encouragement in persuading me that this book would become a reality. Without her you would not now be reading these words.

S.B.Publications publish a wide range of local history books on Norfolk and around the country.

NORFOLK:

Norwich, Volumes 1, 2, 3 & 4

Norwich City F.C.

The Norfolk Broads

Great Yarmouth, Volumes 1 & 2

Norfolk's Railways, Vol.1 – G.E.R.

Norfolk's Railways, Vol.2 – M. & G.N.

Sheringham & Beeston

Swaffham to Fakenham

Herring Heydays

SUFFOLK:

East Suffolk

West Suffolk

Lowestoft, Volumes 1 & 2

Pakefield & Kessingland

Beccles & Bungay

Suffolk's Railways

CAMBRIDGESHIRE:

Peterborough, Vols.1, 2 & 3

Peterborough Then & Now

The Soke of Peterborough

Huntingdonshire Vol.3

Ted Mott's Cambridge

Fen & Marshland Villages

Farming in the Fens

Wicken

Curiosities of Cambridgeshire

Village Signs of North Cambs.

For a full list, write (enclosing S.A.E.) to:
S.B.Publications, ᶜ/ₒ 19 Grove Road, Seaford, East Sussex BN25 1TP.